SOCIAL SKILLS
SIMPLIFIED
Being the Best Me

GRADE
5-6

Revised and Edited by
Pat Hadler – Barnes/Hadler Communications

Design
Ginna Clark – Knee Deep Productions

Illustrations
Anni Matsick

Essential Learning Products
P.O. Box 2590
Columbus, Ohio 43216-2590

Printed in the USA or China
10 9 8 7 6 5 4 3 2 1

Acquiring positive social skills enables children to communicate and interact with each other and with adults in ways that are acceptable, satisfying and pleasurable. Basic social skills fall into four categories:

- Interactions with peers

- Interactions with adults

- Manners and politeness

- Appropriate eating and mealtime behaviors

Social Skills Simplified: Being the Best Me, Grade 5-6 provides children an opportunity to learn, review and polish these skills. Using good social skills helps children improve self-esteem, build confidence in social situations and increase popularity among peers and with adults.

Children learn social skills by observation and imitation of parents, relatives and friends as well as through formal instruction at school, in religious settings and in other groups. *Social Skills Simplified: Being the Best Me, Grade 5-6* allows children to work individually and at their own pace.

A skill is presented then followed by exercises to allow children to practice immediately what they have learned. An Answer Page with appropriate responses to the activities is at the back of this book. After students complete a page, review the answers with them to provide immediate feedback. Allowing ample time for discussion is the best way to ascertain if your students understand the material and are able to internalize the positive character attributes presented.

Encourage parents to reinforce character-building skills at home. If children complete the pages in school, send the completed pages home to parents. Before you begin doing the activities, make a copy of the letter on page ii to send home to each student.

Dear Parents,

Your child is beginning to work on character-building skills using *Social Skills Simplified: Being the Best Me, Grade 5-6*. Some children get along well with peers and adults alike. Others seem to have a social crisis daily. Social interactions are highly complex and don't fall into well-defined levels of skills but their components can be identified. When children discover that social skills can be broken into parts and they can practice and improve their skills, they gain confidence in social situations. Even unpleasant situations don't seem so overwhelming.

The lessons in *Social Skills Simplified: Being the Best Me, Grade 5-6*, provide an age-appropriate outline of social skills. However it's your knowledge as a parent that will help you decide which of your child's skills need improvement. Some children may need to focus on questioning rules, while others need to be encouraged to comply with authority. All children can be encouraged to recognize and verbalize their feelings. This skill is an important element in successful peer and adult relationships.

Complying With Adults' Requests

If there is a test of wills when you ask your child to comply with a request, help him isolate the step that seems to be the source of the problem. Does he give his full attention to the directions? Does he show respect in acknowledging the request? Does he begin the task when asked? Does he have a pleasant tone of voice and positive attitude when doing the task? For example, if your child feels he should have some say in scheduling the time he will do the chore, point out to him that when he is responsive to your requests you are more willing to comply with his requests. You will want to praise him and point out that you are aware that he has changed his behavior. Let him know you'll be more reasonable in allowing him to set his schedule within a time frame you provide.

The Need for Reassurance

Most children want reassurance that they can endure the inevitable ups and downs of friendships. Although it's easy for adults to treat children's friendship issues lightly, it's important to indicate that you recognize the significance of problems they're experiencing. Sometime's it's better to stop teaching and just be the parent who says, "I can see you're sad. I'm sorry."

Praise

One of the best ways to reinforce any skill is to praise a child when he displays behavior that is closer to the ideal. For example, if your child has improved in expressing opinions without being argumentative, you'll want to praise him. However, it's reasonable for you to expect that children of this age will demonstrate the ability to distinguish between appropriate and inappropriate times to disagree with an adult. Prompting your child with "This is not the best time to discuss our disagreement of opinions," and praising him when he waits until an appropriate time, will encourage him even more.

Every child makes mistakes. Helping your child learn to deal responsibly with the results of inappropriate behavior is essential to her maturity. She may find it reassuring to know that accepting consequences can help her to get along with others even when she hasn't always been "The Best Me." Growing up is not easy, and it's wise for adults to remember that it's the child's effort that's most important, not perfection.

If you have any questions about any of these character-building activities, feel free to discuss them with me.

Sincerely,

Introduction

Learning to Be a Good Friend

Adults Are Friends, Too

Answer Key

Meet the Students

You're familiar with rules that apply to games you play with friends. There are also rules that apply to getting along with other people.

Friendships are important to you. If you're like most students, you have probably experienced some difficult times with your friends. Friends can be frustrating at times.

This book will help you decide when to ignore friends' annoying behavior and when to tell them how you feel. You will learn why it's not always "what you say" but "how you say it" that may make a friend angry. You will also practice declining an invitation when you don't want to go somewhere or when you already have other plans.

Now that you are older, you may have noticed that adults treat you differently. You have more freedom and more responsibility. This book suggests some guidelines to help you get along well with adults. You'll practice giving your opinion, making complaints, and questioning rules in ways that older people find acceptable and that feel comfortable to you.

Hi, my name is Tabitha. This is Brianne and Roberto. We're going to tell you about a special day our class has planned to help other students "be the best they can be." Turn the page to see how it all started.

School Project

Making Friends

The first step in getting along with others is making friends. One way to make friends is to talk to kids who have similar interests. Create or find a poster that has one of your interests written on it. Talk to the people who are also interested in that topic.

1. Doing an activity together is a good way to make new friends. Check the activities you enjoy. Compare your list with a new person in your class or a group of your friends.

☐ band   ☐ video games   ☐ soccer   ☐ skiing

☐ chess   ☐ cooking   ☐ football   ☐ dancing

☐ arts and crafts   ☐ orchestra   ☐ basketball   ☐ gymnastics

☐ electronics   ☐ reading   ☐ bicycling   ☐ baseball

☐ cheerleading   ☐ writing   ☐ swimming   ☐ movies

☐ computers   ☐ camping   ☐ hiking   ☐ music

☐ chorus   ☐ rock climbing   ☐ fishing   ☐ singing

☐ drama   ☐ astronomy   ☐ canoeing   ☐ animals

☐ sewing   ☐ horseback riding ☐ diving   ☐ volunteering

Making Friends

Find a classmate who is interested in one of the activities you check on the previous page. Sit with that friend. Pretend that you are meeting for the first time. What will you say? A good place to start is to talk about the activity.

1. Read the example below.

    Activity: _____*Swimming*_____
    a. Hi, my name is Diane.
    b. What's your name?
    c. This is my first year on the team.
    d. Are you new, too?

    Decide who will speak first. Then follow the example.

    Activity: _____
    a. Introduce yourself.
    b. Ask the friend's name.
    c. Tell something about yourself related to the activity.
    d. Ask something about your new friend related to what you said about yourself.

    Now switch roles with your partner.

Once you have met a new friend, you will want to introduce that person to your other friends. For example, Brian is new in the neighborhood. When Kevin meets him, he finds out Brian plays the trumpet. The next day Kevin introduces Brian to his friend, Tyrone, who plays in the band. He says, "Brian, this is my friend Tyrone. He's in the school band and he would like you to join."

2. Form groups of three. Assign parts: Two students play the parts of the students who know each other, and one is the new student.
    a. Have one of the friends and the new student meet for the first time.
    b. Introduce yourself to the new student. Discover the student's name and interests.
    c. Introduce the new student to your friend.

    Change parts so that everyone has a chance to introduce the new student to a friend.

Taking Turns

Answer the questions below.

1. How do you and your friends decide who will go first?

_____

_____

2. If you disagree on what activity to do, how do you decide?

_____

_____

3. How do you feel when friends seem to get their way all the time, and your opinion and interests seem to not count?

_____

_____

4. Todd and some friends are planning a party. Everyone except Alex and Robbie gives ideas for the party. Todd says, "What do you think, Alex?" and "Robbie, do you have any ideas?" List some questions the group could ask so that everyone has a chance to give input.

_____

_____

5. In a group activity do you think it is important for every member to participate?
   ___ Yes   ___ No
   Why? _____

_____

Joining a Group

Some other students are playing games. You want to join. I'm going to give each of you a tip on how to act. Then we'll discuss which one worked best.

1. These are the tips that Brianne gave the students for joining a group. Check the plan you think works best for you.

   a. _____ Sit or stand quietly near the group. Look interested in the game.

   b. _____ Sit or stand quietly near the group. Try to discover what the group is playing and what some of the rules are. Without interrupting the game, say, "Hello," to one of the players. Ask a few questions about the game. Ask if you may take a turn or join in. Accept their answer.

   c. _____ Sit or stand quietly near the group. When you recognize the game, announce to the players that you are also playing.

2. Explain why you think the plan you checked works best.

   _____

   _____

   _____

1. Sometimes a group may not want a student to play with them because that person has caused problems in the past. Name some behaviors that might cause a group not to want a particular student to join them.

   _____

   _____

2. Choose the best word for each blank.

time	because	group	act	show	behavior

   If the **a)**_____ doesn't want to play with you **b)**_____ of the way you **c)**_____, you can look for ways to **d)**_____ that you are trying to change your **e)**_____. Be patient. Show good behavior in other ways. It may take **f)**_____ for the group to trust you again.

3. Sometimes a group may not want anyone new to join them. They may be rude or mean to anyone who tries to join. Name some reasons groups might act this way.

   _____

   _____

4. Choose the best word for each blank.

group	remember	things	part	someone	join

   If a **a)**_____ of people are rude to you when you try to **b)**_____ in an activity, ignore them. Find friends who like to do the same **c)**_____ that you like to do. When **d)**_____ tries to join a group you are in, **e)**_____ how it felt when you wanted to be a **f)**_____ of a group.

Special Needs Friends

This exercise will help you understand the some of the challenges faced by friends with special needs. All of you will be able to complete the obstacle course, but each of you has been assigned a unique challenge. Some can't see the course while others may need help with their crutches. You will need to help one another. The object is to get your whole group through the course.

1. No two people are the same. It's just that some differences are just a little more apparent than others. Everyone has his or her own unique strengths and weaknesses. Below, make a list of things you can do well and things that are hard for you to do.

Things I Do Well   **Things That Are Hard For Me**

_____   _____

_____   _____

_____   _____

_____   _____

2. Sometimes people make fun of others' weaknesses. Why do you think people do this?

_____

_____

3. How could having empathy help a person stop making fun of others?

_____

_____

Empathy

Understanding the feelings of others helps you be a good friend. Look up the word **empathy** in the dictionary. Write the definition on the lines below.

_____

_____

> Sometimes when people are sad, they want to be alone. Sometimes they would rather talk or do something fun. Katie's dog died and she's very sad. Her friends invited her to play kick ball because they know that's her favorite game and it might make her feel better.

Friends share happy times and sad times. The way friends feel may affect the way they act. In each situation below, write what you think the person is feeling. Then write what a friend could do to show he or she cares.

1. Vivian does poorly on a test.
   She's feeling: _____
   A friend's response: _____

2. Antonio gets the lead in the school play.
   He's feeling: _____
   A friend's response: _____

3. Adrienne's grandfather dies.
   She's feeling: _____
   A friend's response: _____

4. Jessica's parents are getting a divorce.
   She's feeling: _____
   A friend's response: _____

Loaning Possessions to Friends

1. Choose the best word for each blank.

>   possessions   return   parents   me   break   valuable

Before you loan a possession to a friend, think is it a)_____? Is it easy to
b)_____? Is it special to c)_____ for some reason? Has this
friend taken care of my d)_____ in the past? Did my e)_____
say I could loan this item? Did we set a time when my friend will f)_____
the possession?

2. Read the stories. Underline the information that will help the person decide whether
   or not to loan a possession. Write what you think the person will do.

   a. Cheryl asks Jocelyn if she can borrow some jewelry. The jewelry Cheryl wants to
      borrow is inexpensive. Cheryl has always taken care of things she has borrowed.
      What do you think Jocelyn will do? _____

   b. Mark sits next to Daniel. Mark never seems to have the supplies he needs to do his
      work. He asks Daniel if he can borrow a pencil again today. What do you think
      Daniel will do? _____

3. List some possessions or situations when you should not share. Explain why
   sharing is not a good idea in that situation.

Situation or Possession	**Reason I Shouldn't Share**
_____	_____
_____	_____
_____	_____

Before you loan any of your
possessions, be sure to ask
yourself these questions:

1. **Is it valuable?**
2. **Can it be easily broken?**
3. **Is it special to me?**
4. **How long have I owned it?**
5. **Has this friend taken
   good care of your
   possessions before?**

Respecting Others' Property

Asking permission before you use something that belongs to someone else shows respect for that person. Taking care of possessions you have borrowed and using public property carefully also shows respect for others.

1. Read the stories and then answer the questions. Underline in each story the information that helps you answer the question. Write your answers on the lines.

   a. Micah needs scissors to complete his social studies project. His teacher is busy working with a group. The classroom supplies are kept in the teacher's closet. What will Micah do?

   _____

   _____

   b. Amanda goes into the girls' bathroom at school. Some younger students have been in the restroom rinsing dirty paint brushes. Paint is splattered over the sinks. What should Amanda do?

   _____

   _____

   c. At recess Robert finds a soccer ball on the playground. The ball is marked to indicate it's the property of the gym teacher. She allows the students to use the gym balls at the lunch break. Robert and his friends want to play soccer. What do they do?

   _____

   _____

2. Answer the questions.
   a. If someone used your possessions without asking, how did you feel about it?

   _____

   b. In what ways can a person show respect for public property?

   _____

   c. List one or two examples from your school or community that show a lack of respect for public property.

   _____

   d. How do you feel about their actions?

   _____

Cheating

Cheating occurs when a person acts dishonestly or misleads others on purpose. Cheating can happen in school, at home or during sports. Sometimes cheating can occur by accident. Most of the time cheating happens because it makes difficult things easier. When people cheat, it's not fair to others.

Choose the best word for each blank.

begin   avoid   politely   understands   stop   clear   everyone

A good way to **a)**_____ problems is to make simple and **b)**_____ rules before you **c)**_____ to play. For example, the rules for the water relay were not complete. One team thought it was fair to run back to the beginning of the line and one team thought they should pass the cup back to the beginning.

When there's confusions about the rules, **d)**_____ and discuss the rules. When everyone **e)**_____ and agrees on the rules, begin again. Then if someone cheats, **f)**_____ tell the person it is more fun to play if **g)**_____ follows the rules.

Answer the questions.

1. What are some ways people cheat?

   _____

   _____

   _____

2. Why do people cheat?

   _____

   _____

   _____

3. How does cheating keep a person from getting along with others?

   _____

   _____

   _____

4. Brianne suggests that when a friend cheats, you should first remind the person of the rules. Would you remind the person of the rules or call the person a "cheater?" Explain your choice.

   _____

   _____

   _____

5. Alice sits beside Raymond. She didn't do her homework last night. She asks Raymond if she may copy his answers before the teacher collects the papers. What should Raymond do?

   _____

   _____

   _____

6. Tim is playing a board game with his family. He draws a card that says, "Lose a turn," but he says the card says, "Roll again." His sister sees the card. She says, "Tim cheated." What should Tim do?

   _____

   _____

   _____

7. Katelyn studied hard for her geography quiz, but she forgets the names of two countries. Her study sheet is in her desk. What should Katelyn do?

   _____

   _____

   _____

Disagreements with Friends

When you disagree with a friend, politely tell your friend how you feel. Then remember to listen to how your friend feels. Try to understand his or her point of view. Remember that your friendship is more important than one disagreement.

1. Choose the best word for each blank.

feel   everything   agree   listen   disagree

It's not only okay, but quite normal to **a)**_____ with others. You don't have to agree on **b)**_____ to be friends with someone. When you disagree, say how you **c)**_____. Then **d)**_____ to how the other person feels. You need to **e)**_____ to disagree.

Sometimes when you disagree with a friend, you might state your feelings too harshly. You may put down your friend's idea because you disagree. You might have hurt your friend's feelings. This is a good time to use the words, "I'm sorry."

2. Check the blank if a person should apologize. Underline the name of the person who should say, "I'm sorry."

a. _____ James and Mitchell walk to school together. Mitchell overslept. He rushed to get ready for school. When he got to their meeting place, James was still there. The boys got a tardy slip at school.

b. _____ Claire bought the same top that Erin bought the day before. Claire wore the top to school before Erin did, and everyone liked it. Erin got mad at Claire.

c. _____ Emily and JoAnn are good friends. Emily doesn't like it when JoAnn plays with others girls. Maggie invites JoAnn to play after school, and Emily gets mad. She says, "Go ahead. See if I care." JoAnn explains to Emily that she likes her, but she also wants to play with other friends.

d. _____ Kyle likes one professional baseball team. Peter likes another. Both teams make it to the World Series. Peter explains why he thinks his team will win. Kyle says, "We'll just have to see how the series turns out."

Our class has learned that even when you follow rules for getting along with others, you still might disagree with friends. And there may be times when you will need to say, "I'm sorry."

Saying "No"

There are times when your friends may ask you to do things you know are wrong Sometimes you may be with a group when someone does something you know is wrong. You may be afraid your friends will be angry or make fun of you if you say, "I'm not going to do that." It's hard to say no but you can feel proud when you do.

Check the stories below in which the person should say, "No." Underline the parts of the sentence(s) that help you decide between simply disagreeing with friends and saying, "No."

1. _____ Bill invites some friends to sleep over at his house. The boys plan a pillow fight. Jim whispers to George, "I brought two hockey pucks. You can have one. Put it in your pillow and we'll give the other guys a jolt."

2. _____ Lucy and Hiroko are trying to decide what they will do on Saturday. Lucy wants to go to the park. Hiroko wants to go to a movie. Lucy tries to convince Hiroko to do what she wants to do.

3. _____ Yvette and her friends are walking home after school. They see water in a ditch that has partially frozen. Some of the girls begin skating on the ice. They ask Yvette to join them.

4. _____ After they eat lunch, David and Josh go back to the classroom. The teacher is gone, but the test they will take is right on her desk in plain view. Josh tells David to keep an eye out, and he will copy the test questions.

5. _____ Taylor and Jack are at Taylor's house after school listening music. Taylor loves country music but Jack prefers rock and roll. Taylor insists on listening to his music.

The purpose of this activity is to give you practice in saying no. When your friends ask you to do things you know you shouldn't do or to do things you don't want to do, say no. What do a lot of people say in order to get others to do what they want?

Come on. No one will know.

You think you are better than everyone else.

Chicken!

Wimp!

Let's try and do it just once.

Ignoring Friends' Behavior

Sometimes people do things just to make you angry or to get you in trouble. But sometimes they may not be aware that they are bothering you. The best thing to do is ignore them.

Read the story below, then make your choices.

Eric is reading quietly in the classroom. Mr. Davis, the teacher, is working at his desk. The other students are involved in their work. Roy throws an eraser at Eric.

Choose either **a** or **b.** See what happens.

a. Eric ignores Roy. (Now read **3.**)

b. Eric picks up the eraser and throws it back at Roy. (Now read **2.**)

   1) Mr. Davis says, "Go to the principal's office, Eric. I'll meet you there when the bell rings." Roy give Eric an exaggerated look of sympathy. (No matter what you think Eric should do, he must ignore Roy or this is not going to end—at least, it will not end in a good way for Eric.)

   2) Mr. Davis looks up just as Eric throws the eraser. He asks Eric to come to his desk. Eric looks over at Roy who is laughing. (If you think Eric should ignore Roy, read **3.** If you think Eric should step on Roy's foot as he walks by, read **5.**)

   3) Roy goes back to reading also.

   4) Mr. Davis says, "Eric, go back to your desk. We'll talk when the bell rings." Roy grins at Eric. (If you think Eric should ignore Roy, read **3.** If you think Eric should shove Roy, read **1.**)

   5) Roy says, "Ouch! Eric stepped on my foot on purpose." Under his breath he calls Eric a name. (If you think Eric should ignore Roy, read **3.** If you think Eric should call Roy a name, read **4.**)

Giving Feedback

There are times when you need to let others know they are bothering you or their behavior is annoying. This is called constructive criticism or giving feedback, and learning to do it in ways that aren't hurtful can be a challenging skill. Following these steps may help.

1. Choose the best word for each blank.

chance	**feel**	**describe**	**understand**	**respond**	**bothers**

Recognize when something **a)**_____ you. Think: "How does that make me **b)**_____?" Talk to the person and **c)**_____ the behavior that is bothering you. Explain how the behavior makes you feel or how others **d)**_____ to the behavior. Give the person a **e)**_____ to talk. Listen to what the friend has to say. Try to **f)**_____ that person's feelings.

2. Read the stories below. Then describe the feedback you think the friend should say.

a. Katrina constantly complains about the way she looks. She says, "My hair looks awful," or "I'm so fat," or "I'm ugly." Natalie and her other friends try to say nice things to help Katrina feel better, but they are tired of Katrina's comments. Some of the girls avoid sitting by her. Natalie decides to talk to Katrina. What do you think Natalie will say?

_____

_____

_____

b. Greg invites some friends to his house. When they play video games, Greg says, "I get to play every time because it's my game." When they go outside to play football, Greg says, "I'm quarterback because it's my football." Soon the boys go home. Henry stays. He talks to Greg about why the other boys left so early. What do you think Henry will say?

_____

_____

_____

c. Jeremy never takes his gym clothes home to be washed because he keeps forgetting. As a result, he always smells during gym class. That makes others not want to be around him because they are bothered by the smell. Tyler decides to talk to Jeremy about it. What should Tyler say?

_____

_____

_____

Ignore Annoying Behavior or Give Feedback?

We have talked about two ways to deal with annoying behavior. How do you decide if you will 1) ignore the behavior, or 2) give negative feedback?

Read the examples below. Place the number of each example on the diagram below. Where you place the number depends on how you think the person whose name is underlined should respond. You might feel two ways at the same time in some situations. Put those numbers in the overlapping area. The first one is done for you. Discuss your answers with a friend. Explain your decisions.

1. Tara often forgets to bring home from school the books that she needs. She asks <u>Meredith</u> if she can borrow hers.

2. <u>Logan</u> gets angry easily. Aaron knows this and calls Logan a wimp.

3. <u>Greta</u> whistles while she reads. Rachel cannot concentrate when Greta whistles.

4. Thomas frequently asks <u>John</u> for paper and pencil.

5. <u>Maria</u> sits beside Sally. Sally twirls her hair. It annoys Maria.

6. When Cody sees a friend's snack, he asks if he can have some. Lately, <u>Will</u> and other friends have avoided sitting next to Cody.

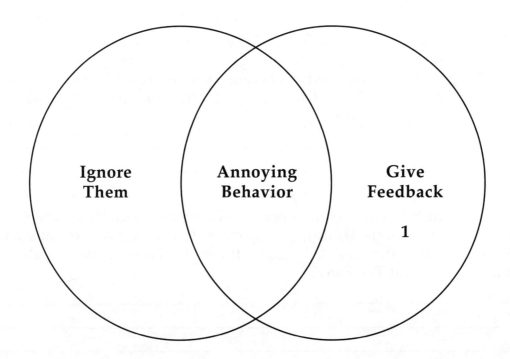

Standing Up for Your Rights

All people are important. This means you are important, too. Sometimes others may not treat you that way. They may speak rudely to you, boss you around, or use your possessions without asking. There are times when you must stand up for your rights.

STEPS FOR STANDING UP FOR YOUR RIGHTS

1. **Think about how you feel.**
2. **Tell the person what bothers you as soon as it happens.**
3. **Say how the incident made you feel.**
4. **Say what you wish the other person would do next time.**
5. **Listen to the person's answer. Sometimes friends may not know how you feel. They may want to apologize.**

Zane, Ian, and Miguel are working on a group report. Each boy selects a topic. When they get together to organize the report, Ian and Miguel don't have their parts. The group loses points because they missed the deadline for their rough draft.

What should Zane say to stand up for his rights? Reread the steps above. Fill in the blanks.

1. It bothered me when you_____.

2. I feel _____

   when you _____.

3. The next time we have a group assignment I wish you would _____

   _____

Then Zane listens to his friends.

4. Do you think they will be more responsible next time? ____ Yes ____ No

5. Have you ever stood up for your rights? ____ Yes ____ No

6. Did you feel better after you talked with the other person? ____ Yes ____ No

7. Why do you think you did or didn't feel better?

   _____

   _____

Nonverbal Communication

Nonverbal communication is communication with actions and expressions, rather than with words. You can communicate a lot of information with just your eyes and your gestures.

1. Work with a friend. Select a situation and communicate it to your friend. See if they can guess what situation your chose. Take turns.

   a. Just when you sit down to watch your favorite television program, your mom tells you to clean your room.

   b. Your teacher is writing the homework assignment on the board. You estimate it will take you at least two hours to do all of it.

   c. You just learned your best friend is moving.

   d. You are the goalie on your soccer team. The other team scores a point you think you could have prevented.

   e. You are almost at school when you realize you forgot your instrument for band practice.

   f. You realize someone has taken things out of your desk.

2. Read the stories below. Write how you think the person whose name is underlined will respond to the other person's nonverbal communication.

   a. The <u>teacher</u> is talking to Danielle about the assignments she has not completed. Danielle rolls her eyes while the teacher is talking.

   _____

   b. <u>Debra</u> sinks two foul shots in her team's championship game. Betty gives her a "high five."

   _____

   c. <u>Paul</u> is runner-up in the school spelling bee. Paul's teacher sees him sitting alone. He sits beside Paul and pats him on the back.

   _____

   d. <u>Sarah</u> tells her younger sister, Mia, that she can't borrow her CD player. Mia slams the door when she leaves the room.

   _____

We're going to try communicating without speaking! Everyone get in pairs. One person selects one of the situations listed, then act out the situation. See if your partner guesses what you're trying to communicate.

Put Downs

Sometimes you may call someone a name or use a put down when something else is really bothering you. Before you call someone a name, think about what the real problem is. If it seems like it's an appropriate time, tell the person how you feel. You may feel jealous, disappointed in yourself, or confused about something. Talk about your feelings without blaming someone else.

Read the stories. Describe what you think the person whose name is underlined is feeling.

1. Fiona sits next to Charlie. When the teacher is with another group, Charlie makes faces and noises at her. Fiona stops herself before she calls Charlie a name. What do you think Fiona is feeling?

   _____

2. Alicia comes to school with a new coat. All of her friends admire it. Veronica wanted a coat like it. Veronica thinks about what she is feeling. She decides not to talk about Alicia behind her back. What do you think Veronica is feeling?

   _____

3. Patrick and Harry used to be close friends. Now Harry is playing with some older boys. He doesn't ask Patrick to join them. How do you think Patrick is feeling?

   _____

Fiona, Veronica, and Patrick might have called someone a name, but they didn't. Instead, they stopped long enough to think about what they were feeling.

Choose one of the stories. Write what the student could say instead of calling someone a name.

_____ could say, "I feel _____ because
_____ ."

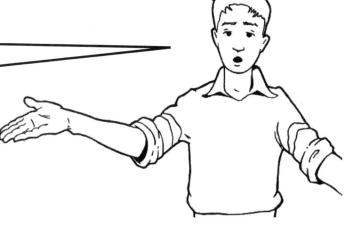

Words such as stuck-up, jerk, weirdo, baby, and wimp are put downs. Our class got along better when we agreed to stop calling each other names and talk about what was really bothering us.

Declining Invitations

If a friend invites you to do something you don't want to do, or you know your parents won't let you, thank the friend for the invitation and tell the friend you can't participate. Then say that you would like to do something with the friend at another time.

If you get invited to do something but you already have other plans, explain the situation to your friend. If you must decline an invitation, be sure to do it as soon as possible so your friend can invite someone else. Never agree to do something with one friend, and then cancel the plans to do something else with another friend.

1. Choose the best word for each blank.

   friend   situation   won't   participate   decline   another

   If a **a)**_____ invites you to do something, and you don't want to do it, or your parents **b)**_____ let you, thank the friend for the invitation. Tell the friend you can't **c)**_____. Then say you would like to do something else with the friend **d)**_____ time. If you have other plans, explain the **e)**_____ to your friend. If you want to and it's possible, include your friend in your plans. If you must **f)**_____ an invitation, be sure to do it as soon as possible so your friend may invite someone else.

2. Read the following stories. Write a polite way for the person to decline the invitation.

   a. Jerry asks Doug to play basketball after school. Doug has promised a neighbor that he will help unload wood. Doug says:

   _____

   _____

   b. Mary invites Elaine to go to the circus with her family. Elaine and her family will be out of town that day. Elaine says:

   _____

   _____

   c. Ned accepted an invitation to go camping with Mark's family. Later, Adam invited Ned to go to an amusement park on the same day. Ned would rather go to the amusement park. What do you think Ned should do?

   _____

   _____

Giving and Receiving Compliments

You can make other people feel good when you say something nice about them or what they did. It shows other people that you notice them and their accomplishments. It's nice to hear compliments from others. But when someone gives you a compliment you may feel embarrassed and not know what to say. It's polite to say, "Thank you."

1. Read the situations below. Write a compliment that a friend might give.

   a. Sean has new glasses.

   _____

   b. Mario wins the school's sportsmanship award.

   _____

   c. Dean got a new watch.

   _____

   d. April plays a duet in the spring concert.

   _____

2. If the person whose name is underlined seems embarrassed by the compliment, write **E** in the blank; write **D** if the person disagrees; and write **A** if the person accepts the compliment.

   a. _____ Chris improves his math grade. Craig says, "Way to go, Chris!" Chris says, "Yeah, but my social studies grade stinks."

   b. _____ Kori's grandmother visits the school's art show. Afterward she says, "Kori, your work is good. I really like your pen-and-ink owl sketch." Kori replies, "Thanks, I like that one, too."

   c. _____ Jeremy sings a solo in the holiday concert. The principal sees him walking out the door. He says, "You did a great job today, Jeremy." Jeremy pretends he doesn't hear him.

   d. _____ Maureen has new earrings. Cara says, "Your earrings are cute." Maureen says, "Thanks, I got them at the mall."

   > Giving a compliment to a friend shows you care, and makes them feel good.

Mealtime Manners

The way you eat your food and conduct yourself at the table says a lot about the kind of person you are. Mealtime can be a great, fun time to eat and socialize, or it can be uncomfortable and troublesome. A lot depends on how you act, and how well you remember your manners.

Answer the questions below.

1. Describe the way you and your friends act in the lunchroom:

   _____

   At home: _____

   _____

2. How is your behavior different in different places?

   _____

3. What behaviors of other people annoy you at mealtime?

   _____

4. Why is it important to have good mealtime behavior?

   _____

Lunchtime doesn't have to be the worst part of the day!

Being Introduced to an Adult

When you are introduced to an adult, you can shake hands and say "Hello," or, "I'm glad to meet you." Adults may want to talk to you. You can help keep the conversation going by giving more than one-word answers.

1. Choose the best word for each blank.

   compliment   introduced   nice   conversation   start   before

   When you are **a)**_____ to an adult, you can shake hands and say, "Hello," or "It's **b)**_____ to meet you." The person may want to talk to you. If you have heard about her or him **c)**_____ you meet, you may want to say something nice such as Roberto did when he met Mr. Phelps. You may want to **d)**_____ the person on a talent or work that he or she does. This is one way to **e)**_____ a conversation. If the person asks you questions, you can keep the **f)**_____ going by giving more than one-word answers.

2. Read the situations below and describe what you would say if you were introduced to the adult mentioned in each situation.

   a. Leslie and Jeanne ride to the tennis court. Mrs. Kraft, Leslie's new band teacher, is walking off the court. Leslie has told Jeanne that not only is Mrs. Kraft a good band instructor, but she is a good flutist as well. When Leslie introduces Jeanne to Mrs. Kraft, Jeanne says,

   _____

   b. Bill and Brett were throwing the ball in the front yard when Bill's new neighbor, Jon, pulled into the driveway next door. Bill had already told Brett that Jon was studying music in college, and played the drums on the weekends with a local band. When Bill introduces Brett to his neighbor Jon, what should Brett say?

   _____

Getting Along with Adults

Answer the questions.

1. What did the class say are the three key qualities they have discovered for getting along with adults?
   1. _____ 2. _____ 3. _____

2. Think about and describe a situation when you had difficulty getting along with an adult. What would have helped you get along better?

   _____

   _____

3. Take a poll of adults you know. Ask, "What qualities of kids help adults and kids get along best?" Fill in the graph below.

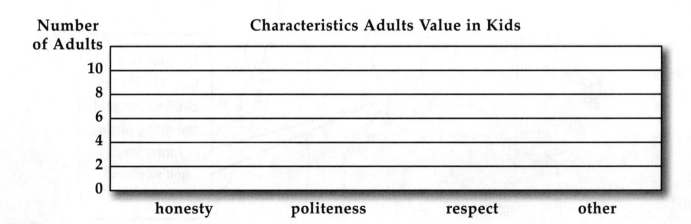

Conversation

It's easy to keep a conversation going. When you are asked a question, answer it. Then ask a question or make a comment about the same subject. That's the way a conversation works. Fill in the blanks or ask a friend to read the parts with you aloud.

Roberto: I'm glad to meet you, Mr. Phelps. Brianne said you tell funny jokes.

Mr. Phelps: I'm glad to meet you, Roberto. I hear you write funny stories.

Roberto: _____

                    _____

Mr. Phelps: _____

                    _____

Roberto: _____

                    _____

Brianne: We need to go now, Roberto. Mom said to be home by 5 o'clock.

Roberto: Goodbye, Mr. Phelps. I look forward to hearing your next new joke.

Imagine your favorite author, television star, or athlete is visiting your city. You have a chance to talk to the person and get an autograph. See if you can "keep the conversation going." You may want to start with something like: "I've been looking forward to meeting you" and then follow with a compliment about the person's talents."

The person's name: _____

Favorite person says, "Hi, what's your name?"

You say, _____ .

Favorite person says, _____ .

You ask, _____ ?

Favorite person answers, _____

and then asks, _____ ?

You answer, _____ .

Thank you for your time. I should be going. Other people are waiting to talk to you.

Being Honest

Telling the truth is difficult especially when you know you will be punished for
something. But it's good to remember that people are more likely to trust you if they
know you always tell the truth. And adults often punish less severely when you are
truthful from the start.

1. Carol asks her mother if she may walk to the store. Her mother says, "No." Later
   Carol's neighbor, Heather, invites her to come over. The girls ask Heather's father if
   they may go to the store. He says, "Yes." Carol's mother sees them returning. When
   Carol gets home, her mother asks Carol where they went.

   What should Carol say?

   _____

   _____

   Explain your answer.

   _____

   _____

2. Darren helps the gym teacher, Mrs. Hunter, after school. While Mrs. Hunter is in her
   office, Bobby drops by to say "Hello" to Darren. When the boys try to see if they can
   jump and reach above the volleyball net, they accidentally tear it. The next day Mrs.
   Hunter asks Darren if he knows anything about the torn volleyball net.

   What should Darren say?

   _____

   _____

   Explain your answer.

   _____

   _____

   Do you think Mrs. Hunter might have acted differently if Darren had told her about
   tearing the net when it happened?   ____ Yes   ____ No

   Why or why not?

   _____

   _____

Accepting Consequences

When you do something (cause), there's a consequence (effect) for your behavior. Consequences may be good or bad. Consequences help you decide if you want to act the same way again.

1. Underline the cause and circle the consequence.

   a. Ryan's father asks him to vacuum the living room and straighten the coat rack while he goes to the store. Ryan completes the chores with no complaints. When his father returns, he smiles at Ryan and says, "Good job. That was a big help!"

   b. Jamie is watching television. Her sister, Rosie, asks for help with her homework. Jamie says, "I'm too tired." Later, when Janie asks Rosie to go bike riding with her, Rosie says, "No."

2. Read the story. Check the best answer.

   The class is reading quietly. Eva begins to cry. Mr. Ford asks what's wrong. Eva shows him a nasty note that Elizabeth has written. Mr. Ford asks Elizabeth to stay after the bell rings.

   a. _____ Elizabeth says, "It was Eva's fault. She has turned all my friends against me. I tried to talk to her but she won't listen. "

   b. _____ Elizabeth says, "I was wrong to write the note. I'm sorry. May I tell you what happened first?"

3. Choose the best word for each blank.

caused	your	fault	easier	part

   Sometimes it may be hard for you to see that your actions a)_____
   something to happen. It's often b)_____ to see how a friend caused you to
   do something. It may seem to you that the consequence is the friend's
   c)_____. Even if a friend had a d)_____ in what you did,
   it's important to accept the consequences for e)_____ actions.

Asking Favors

There are times when everyone needs help. When you ask a person to do a favor, you are asking the person to do something special and out of the ordinary.

1. Choose the best word for each blank.

   why   please   help   accept   ask   thank   advance

   When you need **a)**_____, decide who you will **b)**_____.
   Your decision may depend on who knows the most about the subject, who is available, or who is most likely to help you. Explain **c)**_____ you need the person's help and remember to say **d)** "_____" when you ask. Also, remember to ask in **e)**_____ so the person has time to do what you ask. If the answer is "Yes," **f)**_____ the person for agreeing to help. Be willing to help when this person asks you to do a favor in return. If the person says "No," **g)**_____ the decision graciously.

2. Think of a time when you may need to ask a favor.

   What help might you need? _____

   Who will you ask? _____

   Why? _____

   How far in advance should you ask? _____

   What will you say? _____

   If the person agrees, what will you say? _____

   If the person is not able to help you, what will you do? _____

Helping Others

Adults appreciate help, too. Some may have disabilities or need help in some way.

1. Answer the questions.
    a. Mrs. Lane has a two-year-old. She is expecting another baby soon. Tyrone lives next door. What could Tyrone do to help Mrs. Lane?

    _____

    b. Tori's teacher Mr. Carter is in a wheelchair. One day he was trying to go down the hall while balancing a stack of books on his lap. How could she help Mr. Carter?

    _____

    c. Keith lives next door to Mr. Stone who is elderly and has difficulty getting around. What are some things Keith could do to help?

    _____

    d. Joyce's mother is studying for a nursing exam. It's time for Joyce's little sister to go to bed. What could Joyce do to help?

    _____

    e. Bella is at the mall. She sees her mother's friend, Mrs. Tucker, on crutches and with several packages. What could Bella do to help?

    _____

2. Think of people you know who have some type of special needs. Make a list.

Special Need	What You Could Do To Help
_____	_____
_____	_____
_____	_____
_____	_____
_____	_____

3. Answer the questions.
    a. Describe how you react when an adult asks you to put away groceries, watch a younger child, wash the chalkboard, or do other chores.

    _____

    b. What jobs do you expect to be paid for doing?

    _____

    c. What jobs do you think of as favors and for which you don't expect to be paid?

    _____

Complying with Requests

Sometimes parents, teachers, and other grownups will request that you do something, or expect you to follow directions. It's important to follow through with what is asked of you.

> Sometimes adults count on kids to help them.
> There are lots of chores and jobs we can do.
> When adults ask for help, follow these steps.

STEPS FOR MEETING ADULTS' REQUESTS

1. **Stop what you are doing and listen carefully.**
2. **Let the person know you heard the request. Say "Yes" or "OK."**
3. **If you don't understand, ask the adult to explain it again.**
4. **Begin the job right away, or ask the adult if you may do the task at a later time.**
5. **If the adult says the job must be done now, do it right away.**
6. **Have a pleasant voice and a positive attitude when you talk with adults.**

Getting along with adults is important, especially when they ask you to do things. Read the story below. Look at the steps above. Explain how Trent could have avoided problems with his dad.

Trent is shooting baskets. Before he leaves, Trent's dad asks him to do a few chores. Trent continues to shoot baskets while his dad talks. When his dad is finished talking and gets ready to leave, Trent says, "Sure." Later, when his father returns home, Trent is still shooting baskets. Trent is grounded for the next day.

_____

_____

_____

_____

_____

Have you ever followed all the steps for complying with requests and still gotten into trouble? The problem may have been your attitude or tone of voice, or the way you did the job. You may want to disagree, question, or postpone a request sometimes. Try to remember that adults will be more likely to listen to you if you have cooperated with their requests in the past.

Find a partner. Act out the scene below. First, read Grace's lines in a way that would make her mother angry. Then read them so that her mother will be pleased.

Mother: Grace, will you please pick up the twigs in the front yard before I mow the grass?

Grace: Should I pick up twigs this small? (She holds up a tiny twig.)

Mother: No. (Her mother holds up a larger twig.) Pick up ones this size and larger.

Grace: Okay. (Grace begins to pick up the twigs.)

1. What made the difference in the outcome each time you read the lines?

_____

_____

2. Write a scene like the one above in which the person complies with an adult's request for help. Read the parts with a friend. Try different tones of voice and attitudes to produce different results.

_____

_____

_____

_____

_____

_____

_____

_____

Accepting Criticism

When people criticize you, it doesn't mean they don't like you. The criticism is meant to
help you change or improve a behavior.

1. Choose the best word for each blank.

 improve   another   criticism   repeat   carefully

Constructive criticism is often meant to help you **a)**_____. Listen
b)_____ to what the person says. If you don't understand, ask the person
to **c)**_____ it or explain it in **d)**_____ way. Think about how
you can learn from the **e)**_____.

2. Read the stories. Underline the behavior that the criticism is meant to improve or
 change.

 a. The teacher returned Anna's paper. The teacher had written, "Your handwriting is
 excellent, but it is too small to read easily."

 b. At breakfast, Bill's mother noticed the dishes stacked on the counter. She said, "I
 think you forgot the rule that you are responsible for your own dirty dishes."

 c. Julie missed another grounder in softball practice. Julie's coach said, "You've got to
 get behind the ball, Julie. Make sure you've got it before you worry about throwing
 it."

 d. Aaron's teacher spoke to him after school. She said, "I know you often think of
 funny things to say, but you must learn that there are appropriate times to say them
 and there are times when you must keep your thoughts to yourself."

 e. Choose one of the criticisms above. Describe how the person will act or perform if
 he or she does not learn from the criticism.

 _____

 _____

 _____

 _____

Stating Your Opinion

An opinion is the way you think or feel about something. An opinion is not right or wrong, but there is a right way to express your opinion. Even if your opinion is different from another person's, it doesn't mean the other person's opinion is wrong or of any less value than your opinion.

1. Choose the best word for each blank.

right   **opinion**   **Don't**   **disagree**

When you give an **a)**_____, start with "I feel" or "I think."
b)_____ attack or put down other people for their opinions. You may
c)_____, but you both have a **d)**_____ to your opinions.

2. Choose three of the topics listed below. Write an opinion you could share with a friend. Remember to start your opinion with "I think" or "I feel."

video game   **school**   **subject**   **book**   **sport**   **movie**

a. Subject _____

_____

_____

b. Subject _____

_____

_____

c. Subject _____

_____

_____

d. Why do you think people with different opinions sometimes argue?

_____

_____

Disagreeing with Adults

You have a right to disagree with adults, but there are good ways to do this.

1. Choose the best word for each blank.

   adult's   opinion   different   courteous   best   start

   Everyone is entitled to an **a)**_____. Sometimes your opinion may be the same as others; sometimes it will be **b)**_____. When your opinion is different from an adult's opinion, ask yourself, "Is this the **c)**_____ time to state my opinion? Would another time be better to discuss this?"

   If you decide this is a good time to give your opinion, **d)**_____ with "I think" or "I feel." Remember to be **e)**_____ and respectful when you speak. Listen attentively to the **f)**_____ opinion.

2. Read the story then answer the questions below.

   Renee's mother and her friends are working on plans for the school fair. Renee and her friend Christina interrupt to ask if the may walk to the mall. Renee's mother says, "No, I think you are too young to walk to the mall alone." Renee disagrees with her mother.

   a. Is this a good time for Renee to express her opinion? ____ Yes ____ No
      Why or why not?

      _____

   b. What should Renee say to her mother? State her opinion with "I think" or "I feel."

      _____

   c. In what ways can Renee show respect when she give her opinion?

      _____

   d. After Renee states her opinions, what should she do?

      _____

Questioning Rules

Some rules keep you safe. Other rules are made so that everyone is treated fairly. When a rule seems unfair, you may want to change the rule. Keep in mind that often adults feel the most rules are fair and don't need changing. Be ready to accept their answer.

Sometimes rules are made to help you get along with others. Some rules help keep you safe. Other rules are made so that everyone is treated fairly. When a rule seems unfair, you may want to change the rule. The class thought a rule was unfair. Read to find out what they did.

These are the steps they followed:

1. Check with the adult in charge to make sure you understand the rule.

2. Think about why you don't agree with the rule. How do you feel?

3. Think about the purpose of the rule. Does it keep people safe? Does it help them get along with others? Does it guarantee that everyone will be treated fairly?

4. Think about the ways you would change the rule. Remember, the rule should be fair to everyone, not just you.

5. After you follow Steps 1, 2, and 3, do you still think the rule is unfair? If your answer is, "Yes," take action. Talk to the person in charge. Tell the person how you feel about the rule and how you would like to see it changed.

6. Sometimes adults are able to change rules, but sometimes they feel the rule is best the way it is. Be ready to accept their answer.

Read the steps for questioning a rule on the previous page. What should Roberto do if he wants to change the rule? Fill in the blanks.

1. Mrs. Morris, the principal, made the rule. Roberto and his friends think this is the rule: No children are allowed to remain on the school grounds after school is dismissed. Roberto follows **Step 1**. He _____

   _____

   Mrs. Morris says Roberto understands the rule correctly. She explains that the rule was made because there is no supervision for the children after school.

2. Roberto follows **Step 2**. He thinks, the rule bothers him because _____

   _____ .

   The rule makes him feel _____

   _____ .

3. Roberto follows **Step 3**. He thinks, the rule was made to _____

   _____ .

4. Roberto follows **Steps 4**. He understands that children cannot play on the school grounds without supervision, but he wonders if other children and adults would be interested in a program that would provide activities for students after school.

5. Roberto follows **Step 5**. He decides to take action. Check the actions that might help Roberto get the rule changed.

   a. _____ Roberto talks to other students and parents about his ideas. Some of them say they will help him.

   b. _____ Tabitha and Brianne survey the students. They ask how many would stay for an after-school program.

   c. _____ Roberto talks to his friends. He says, "The rule is so dumb. There's no other place to play basketball after school."

   d. _____ A group of students go to the school's parent organization. They agree to help the students.

   e. _____ Roberto's friends make posters that say, "Students have rights, too. Open the basketball courts after school."

Mrs. Morris invites a group of parents, Roberto, and his friends to a meeting. Roberto shows them the results of the survey. They brainstorm to find ways they could get adult supervision.

6. Roberto and his friends follow **Step 6**. They know that in spite of their efforts, it may not be possible to change the rule. No matter the outcome, Roberto taught his class something important about trying to change rules.

7. Write a home or school rule that you would like to change.

   _____

   _____ .

8. Have you talked with the adult in charge to make sure you understand the rule?
   ____ Yes ____ No

9. What bothers you about the rule?

   _____

   _____ .

10. How would you change the rule? Remember, the rule should be fair to everyone, not just you.

    _____ .

Making Complaints

Sometimes you may not want to change a rule, but you would like to say how you feel about it. Maybe you have tried to ignore another student who bothers you, but it hasn't worked. Maybe you might have been treated rudely by a store clerk, and perhaps you would like to make a complaint.

1. Choose the best word for each blank.

   accept   **charge**   **feeling**   **upset**   **good**

   Think about what you are a)_____ and why you feel that way. Identify the person in b)_____. Ask the person to discuss the problem with you. If this isn't a c)_____ time, ask when the person could speak to you. Tell the person why you are d)_____ and how you would like to see the problem handled. Listen carefully to what the adult says. Be prepared to e)_____ the adult's answer.

2. Think of an experience on the playground, in the classroom, at a practice, or at a store that you think is unfair or could be improved. Find a partner. Follow the five steps on the previous page and act out making complaints.

   a.   How is making a complaint different from tattling?

   _____

   _____

   b.   Name two reasons that adults might not listen to a child's complaint.

   _____

   _____

   c.   Why are people your age sometimes afraid to make complaints?

   _____

   _____

Please, Thank You, Excuse Me and You're Welcome

The words "please," "thank you," "excuse me," and "you're welcome" are polite words that show others your appreciation and respect. These are common courtesy words used by people who care about others, and who also care what people think about them.

1. Write an example that shows when it's important to say, "Please."

_____
_____
_____.

2. Write an example that shows when it's important to say, "Thank you."

_____
_____
_____.

3. Write an example that shows when it's important to say, "Excuse me."

_____
_____
_____.

4. Write an example that shows when it's important to say, "You're Welcome."

_____
_____
_____.

We saved this rule for last. Even though you may know this rule, you might forget to use it. Saying, "Please," "Thank you," "Excuse me," and "You're welcome" shows good manners. It also demonstrates politeness and respect. Remember to say these kind words to not only adults, but also your friends.

The Project is Finished!

Review the skills for "Being the Best Me," that Tabitha, Roberto, and Brianne taught the other students.

1. Name two skills that you or your class can do easily.

   _____

   _____

2. Name two skills that you or your class could improve.

   _____

   _____

3. Explain what you will do to improve.

   _____

   _____

4. What were the two most important things you learned?

   _____

   _____

5. Why do you think manners are important?

   _____

   _____

Congratulations, class. Your project isn't something you can see, like the tree the class planted last year, but you certainly did something to improve the school. The faculty and students will remember you for a long time to come.

Being a Good Friend

Page 3
1. Answers will vary.

Page 4
Answers will vary.

Page 5
Answers will vary.

Page 6
1. "b" should be checked.
2. Answers will vary.

Page 7
1. Answers will vary.
2. a. group, b. because, c. act, d. show, e. behavior, f. time
3. Answers will vary.
4. a. group, b. join, c. things, d. someone, e. remember, f. part

Page 8
Answers will vary.

Page 9
Answers will vary.

Page 10
1. a. valuable, b. break, c. me, d. possessions, e. parents, f. return
2. a. "Cheryl has always taken care of things she has borrowed" should be underlined.
   b. "Mark never seems to have the supplies he needs to do his work" should be underlined.
3. Answers will vary.

Page 11
Answers will vary.

Page 12
a. avoid, b. clear, c. begin, d. stop, e. understands, f. politely, g. everyone

Page 13
Answers will vary.

Page 14
1. a, disagree, b. everything, c. feel, d. listen, e. agree
2. "a" should be checked and "Mitchell" underlined.
   "b" should be checked and "Clair" should be underlined.
   "c: should be checked and "Emily" should be underlined.

Page 15
1. Should be checked and "hockey pucks" should be underlined.
3. Should be checked and "some of the girls begin skating on the ice" should be underlined.
4. Should be checked and "he will copy the test questions" should be underlined.

Page 16
Answers will vary.

Page 17
1. a. bothers, b. feel, c. describe, d. respond, e. chance, f. understand
2. Answers will vary.

Page 18
In "Ignore Them" circle, 3 and 5; in "Annoying Behavior circle, 2 and 3; and in "Give Feedback" circle, 1, 4 and 6

Page 19
Answers will vary.

Page 20
Answers will vary.

Page 21
Answers will vary.

Page 22
1. a. friend, b. won't, c. participate, d. another, e. situation, f. decline
2. Answers will vary

Page 23
1. Answers will vary.
2. a. D, b. A, c, E, d. A

Page 24
Answers will vary.

Adults Are Friends, Too

Page 25
1. a. introduced, b. nice, c. before, d. compliment, e. start, f. conversation.
2. Answers will vary.

Page 26
1. honesty, politeness and respect.
2. Answers will vary.
3. Answers will vary.

Page 27
Answers will vary.

Page 28
Answers will vary.

ANSWER KEY

Page 29

1. a. "Ryan completes the chores with no complaints" should be underlined and "Good job" should be circled.

   b. "Jamie says, 'I'm too tired'" should be underlined and "Rosie says no" should be circled.

2. "b" should be checked.

3. a. caused, b. easier, c. fault, d. part, e. your

Page 30

1. a. help, b. ask, c. why, d. please, e. advance, f. thank, g. accept

2. Answers will vary.

Page 31

Answers will vary.

Page 32

Answers will vary.

Page 33

Answers will vary.

Page 34

1. a. improve, b. carefully, c. repeat, d. another, e. criticism

2. a. "it is too small to read easily" should be underlined

   b. "dishes stacked on the counter" should be underlined

   c. "get behind the ball" should be underlined

   d. "there are times when you must keep your thoughts to yourself" should be underlined

   e. Answer will vary.

Page 35

1. a. opinion, b. don't, c. disagree, d. right

2. Answers will vary.

Page 36

1. a. opinion, b. different, c. best, d. start, e. courteous, f. adult's

2. Answers will vary.

Page 38 and 39

Answers will vary.

Page 40

1. a. feeling, b. charge, c. good, d. upset, e. accept

2. Answers will vary.

Page 41

Answers will vary.

Page 42

Answers will vary.